SELECTED PIANO MUSIC

CLARA WIECK SCHUMANN

(1819-1896)

CLARA WIECK SCHUMANN

SELECTED PIANO MUSIC

Quatre Pièces Caractéristiques, Opus 5 (1835-1836)

Soirées Musicales, Opus 6 (1835-1836)

Variations de Concert, Opus 8 (1836-1837)

Scherzo, Opus 10 (1839)

Trois Romances, Opus 11 (1839)

Drei Praeludien und Fugen, Opus 16 (1845)

INTRODUCTION BY
PAMELA SUSSKIND

DA CAPO PRESS • NEW YORK • 1979

Library of Congress Cataloging in Publication Data

Schumann, Clara Josephine Wieck, 1819-1896.
 Selected piano music.

 (Da Capo Press music reprint series)
 Reprint "of the first editions published in Leipzig
and Vienna between 1836 and 1846 by Breitkopf & Härtel,
Hofmeister, and Mechetti."
 CONTENTS: Quatre pieces caractéristiques, op.
5.—Soirées and musicales, op. 6—Variations de concert, op. 8—Scherzo, op. 10—Trois romances, op.
11.—Drei Praeludien und Fugen, op. 16.
 1. Piano music.
M22.S393S9   786.4′05′4   78-31836
ISBN 0-306-79554-X

Da Capo Press Music Reprint Series

This Da Capo Press edition of *Selected Piano Music*
by Clara Schumann is an unabridged republication of the
first editions published in Leipzig and Vienna
between 1836 and 1846 by Breitkopf & Härtel, Hofmeister,
and Mechetti. It is reproduced from originals owned by
the University of California at Berkeley Music Library.

Introduction copyright © 1979 by Pamela Susskind

Published by Da Capo Press, Inc.
A Subsidiary of Plenum Publishing Corporation
227 West 17th Street, New York, N.Y. 10011

INTRODUCTION

Clara Wieck Schumann (1819–1896) occupied a major position in the nineteenth-century musical world. Born in Leipzig on September 13, 1819, the eldest child of the famous pedagogue Friedrich Wieck, she was meticulously trained as a pianist by her father and made a dazzling debut in Leipzig in 1830, at the age of eleven. By 1838 she was renowned throughout Europe for her brilliant technique and uncommon musical sensitivity. She was nominated to the *Gesellschaft der Musikfreunde* and appointed *K.K. Kammervirtuosin* to the Austrian court, an honor rarely bestowed on a foreigner, particularly one so young. Her admirers included Goethe, Grillparzer (whose poem *Clara Wieck und Beethoven* appeared in Vienna in 1838), Chopin, Berlioz, Mendelssohn, and Liszt, who wrote that "her talent delighted me; she had perfect mastery of technique, depth, and sincerity of feeling."[1]

Her triumphs were marred, however, by the development of a bitter dispute with her father. Wieck was violently opposed to her proposed marriage to Robert Schumann, who had come to live with the Wiecks in 1830. The conflict lasted three years. Wieck's objections became increasingly vicious and malevolent; he even attempted to undermine his daughter professionally. In 1840 Clara and Robert took their case to court and finally married, on September 12, 1840.

The couple settled first in Leipzig, moving to Dresden in 1844 and to Düsseldorf in 1850. Marriage posed a number of obstacles to Clara's career: Robert required absolute quiet while composing, and she spent a good deal of time helping him prepare his music for performance. In addition, maternal duties preoccupied her: Marie (b. 1841), Elise (b. 1843), Julie (b. 1845), Emil (b. 1846, d. 1847), Ludwig (b. 1848), Ferdinand (b. 1849), Eugenie (b. 1851), and Felix (b. 1854). Nevertheless she managed to continue playing, and even made tours to Copenhagen (1842) and Russia (1844). Robert's health was another constant difficulty; his erratic nervous system deteriorated gradually until, in 1854, he collapsed completely and was committed to the asylum at Endenich, where he remained until his death in 1856. It was during this time of trouble that the firm friendship between Clara and Johannes Brahms began; Brahms remained a loyal and devoted companion for the rest of her life.

After 1854, in order to support her family, Clara returned to an active concert life. She toured extensively, including another visit to Russia in 1864 and nineteen separate tours to England. In 1857 she moved to Berlin, in 1863 to Baden-Baden; from 1873 to 1878 she resided occasionally in Berlin; and in 1878 she accepted a position as a teacher of piano at Dr. Hoch's Conservatory in Frankfurt. In addition to performing and teaching, she prepared a complete edition of Robert's music (published by Breitkopf and Härtel, 1881–1893), and an edition of his letters from 1827 to 1840, published as *Jugendbriefe* in 1885. She made her last public appearance in 1891, and continued to teach and play for private gatherings until her death on May 20, 1896.

For over half a century, Clara Schumann was indisputably one of the foremost pianists of the time. Eduard Hanslick described an 1856 concert as leaving "an impression of pure satisfaction, experienced when an ideal project is realized harmoniously."[2] Her programs were distinguished

---

[1] Berthold Litzmann, *Clara Schumann: An Artist's Life* (translated and abridged by Grace E. Hadow), London, Macmillan, 1913, Vol. I, p. 201.

[2] Eduard Hanslick, *Music Criticisms, 1846-99* (Henry Pleasants, translator and editor), London, Penguin, 1950, p. 48.

v

by innovative, serious, and sensitive programming. In particular, she introduced the music of Robert Schumann and Johannes Brahms to an often recalcitrant public, and helped to create a wide and appreciative audience for them.

Clara Schumann's enormous achievements as a pianist are well known today. It is less well known, however, that her talents extended to another area: composition. This collection of pieces demonstrates that she was a composer of remarkable promise.

As with her performing career, she began as a child prodigy: her earliest compositions date from 1828. She composed at first in the spirit of all virtuoso pianists, writing glittering bravura pieces designed primarily to show off technical brilliance: polonaises, caprices, a piano concerto, and the ever popular variation-sets based on well-known tunes (the Bellini variations, based on an air from a Bellini opera; the *Souvenir de Vienne*, based on the Kaiser's anthem). The Bellini variation-set, op. 8, written for her first tour to Berlin in 1837, is typical of the style. It overflows with keyboard wizardry—breathtaking flourishes, dazzling arpeggios, and brilliant chromatic runs.

At the same time, she also wrote shorter character pieces, indicative of a deeper musical sensibility: *Quatre pièces caractéristiques,* op. 5, and *Soirées musicales,* op. 6, both written in 1835-36. The first, second, and fourth pieces of the op. 5 set are typical "characteristic" pieces: simple, lively, colorful, often referring to an unusual musical style such as witches' dances or a Spanish caprice. The third piece, the Romance, with its poignant turns from B major to D major, is more original.

The *Soirées musicales,* op. 6, reflect the influence of Chopin and Mendelssohn; but though the overall style might be considered imitative, the pieces show much skill and imagination. The fourth piece, the Ballade, is unusually rich, harmonically and texturally; the first Mazurka bubbles with chromatic turns, unexpected chords, frisky grace notes, rhythmic plays, and phrase elisions.

Robert wrote of the *Soirées*, in the *Neue Zeitschrift* of September 12, 1837, that they contained a "wealth of unconventional resources, an ability to entangle the secret, more deeply twisting threads and then to unravel them."[3] He was sufficiently fond of these pieces to borrow from them: the allegro of his sonata in F# minor, op. 11 (dedicated to Clara), begins with the tritone figure opening her op. 5, no. 4; his Davidsbündler pieces, op. 6, begin with the opening of her second Mazurka, op. 6, no. 5.

During the following years Clara found less time to compose; her strenuous touring schedule, coupled with the troubles with her father, left her little energy. "I should very much like to compose," she wrote to Robert from Vienna in 1838, "but it is quite impossible here. I have to practice in the morning, and till late in the evening we have visitors; by that time my mind is quite exhausted."[4] Only two more pieces were written by 1840, the *Scherzo*, op. 10, and the *Trois Romances*, op. 11.

Both pieces attest to serious artistic purpose. The *Scherzo* is an extremely well constructed piece, based almost entirely on ideas presented in its introduction: running eighth-notes, half-steps surrounding the dominant, chromatic chords, dominant pedal. The dissonant clashes and lucid textures give the piece dramatic energy and coherence; it is easy to understand the piece's popularity. "It is extraordinary to me that my *Scherzo* is so much well-liked here, I always have to repeat it,"[5] Clara wrote to Robert from Paris.

The *Scherzo* was written for the general public; the op. 11 *Romances* were written for herself and Robert. The third romance is particularly imaginative; the first eight bars alone show a

[3] Henry Pleasants, translator and editor, *The Musical World of Robert Schumann, A Selection from his own Writings*, New York, St. Martin's Press, 1965, p. 122.
[4] Litzmann, *op. cit.*, Vol. I, pp. 139-140.
[5] Litzmann, *op. cit.*, Vol. I, p. 242.

remarkable originality, carefully structured and succinctly expressed. All three romances reflect considerable talent, inventiveness, and skill.

After her marriage, Clara found herself faced with a number of new difficulties. At the same time, marriage to Robert presented extraordinary new opportunities: as Robert's wife, she was constantly involved in a rich exchange of ideas; at Robert's instigation, they embarked together on numerous projects of study and composition. One early venture was a joint set of songs, published as his op. 37 (and her op. 12) in 1841; she later published another set of songs, her op. 13. Robert also provided a more indirect inspiration: Clara composed at least one piece every year for him, usually as a birthday gift.

These years bore the richest fruit: her songs, the unpublished *Sonatina*, the three Preludes and Fugues, op. 16, and her Trio, op. 17, as well as the less significant second *Scherzo*, op. 14, and *Quatres pièces caractéristiques,* op. 15. The three Preludes and Fugues, op. 16, basically exercises resulting from a joint study of counterpoint with Robert in 1845, are excellent demonstrations of her skill in writing in an entirely different style.

After 1848, other demands, such as Robert's need for quiet, apparently overwhelmed her. She did not compose again until 1853, when they moved to a new house, with rooms situated so that she could compose without disturbing her husband. That summer she wrote four new pieces, including her variations on a theme of Robert's, op. 20, sketched in time for his birthday, on June 8. These pieces, however, were clearly less serious, written hastily and only for herself and Robert, not destined for public performance.

No new pieces appeared the following year; on Robert's birthday in 1854 he was in the Endenich asylum. Clara's troubles with Robert and, following his death, the necessity of supporting seven children overshadowed any desire to compose. In addition, Robert's death removed one of her principal reasons for composing. After 1853 she never returned to composition.

The irregularity and brevity of her career as a composer may be traced mainly to the obstacles caused by her touring and her marriage. An additional impediment may also be suggested: nineteenth-century attitudes towards women composers. As a composer Clara Schumann met with undeniable prejudice. Her piano concerto, for example, a remarkable work for a fifteen-year-old, was reviewed most offhandedly by C.F. Becker in the February 1837 issue of Schumann's own progressive journal, with the lame disclaimer that little attention need be paid to the piece, "since we are dealing here with the work of a lady."[6] Few of her other pieces were reviewed at all. The influential pianist and conductor Hans von Bülow, a pupil of her father, expressed bitter opposition to women composers: "Reproductive genius can be admitted to the pretty sex, but productive genius unconditionally cannot. . . . There will never be a woman composer, at best a misprinting copyist. . . . I do not believe in the feminine form of the word 'creator.'"[7]

It is obvious from her own writings that she deeply felt the creative instincts of a composer:

There is nothing greater than the joy of composing something oneself, and then listening to it.[8]

Today I once more began . . . for the first time in years, to compose again. . . . Composing gives me great pleasure. . . . When I can work regularly, I feel once more really in my own element. A quite different feeling comes over me, lighter and freer, and everything seems to become bright and cheerful. Music is a large part of my life, and when I must do without it, it is as if I were deprived of bodily and mental vigor.[9]

---

[6] Litzmann, *op. cit.*, Vol. I, p. 96.
[7] Karl-Fritz Bernhardt, "Schumanns Weggefährtin—zur Musikschöpferischen Emanzipation der Frau," in *Musica* X, 1956, p. 461.
[8] Litzmann, *op. cit.*, Vol. I, p. 410.
[9] Litzmann, *op. cit.*, Vol. II, p. 36.

Inevitably, she herself came to believe in society's general expectations. By the time she was twenty, she had already absorbed the commonly held attitudes:

> I once thought that I possessed creative talent, but I have given up this idea; a woman must not desire to compose—not one has been able to do it, and why should I expect to? It would be arrogance, though, indeed, my father led me into it in earlier days.[10]

It is clear that Clara Schumann was exceptionally talented as a composer, and it is unfortunate that her *oeuvre* is limited to scarcely more than thirty pieces. The pieces gathered here show remarkable inventiveness, artistic craft, and subtle originality. They certainly deserve a place in today's repertory.

PAMELA SUSSKIND
Mt. Holyoke College
South Hadley, Mass.
September, 1978

[10] Litzmann, *op. cit.*, Vol. I, p. 259.

THE WORKS OF CLARA SCHUMANN

Op.	Title	scoring	date of composition	date of publication
—	Variationen über ein Tyroler Lied	piano	1830	—
—	Variationen über ein Original-Thema	piano	1830	—
1	Quatre Polonaises	piano	1828–?1830	1830 (Leipzig, Hofmeister)
2	Caprices en forme de valse	piano	by 1833	1832 or 1833 (Leip, Hof)
3	Romance varié	piano	1831	1833 (Leip, Hof)
—	Rondo in B minor	piano	1833	—
4	Valses romantiques	piano	?1833	? (Leip, Hof)
—	"An Alexis"	voice and piano	1833	—
—	"Walzer" (F. Lyser)	voice and piano	1834	—
5	Quatre pièces caractéristiques Impromptu: le sabbat Caprices à la Boleros Romance Scène fantastique: Le Ballet des Revenants	piano	1835 or 1836	1839 (Leip, Hof)
6	Soirées musicales Toccatina Notturno Mazurka Ballade Mazurka Polonaise	piano	1835 or 1836	1836 (Leip, Hof)
7	Premier concert, A mi	piano and orchestra	1835 or 1836	1836 (Leip, Hof)
8	Variations de concert, sur la cavatine du Pirate, de Bellini, C ma	piano	1836–1837	1837 (Vienna, Haslinger)

Op.	Title	scoring	date of composition	date of publication
9	Souvenir de Vienne, G ma	piano	1837 or 1838	1838 (Vienna, Diabelli)
10	Scherzo, D mi	piano	by 1839	1838 or 1839 (Leip, Breitkopf & Härtel)
11	Trois Romances, (E flat mi, G mi, A flat ma) [G minor Romance also published separately, as the *Andante und Allegro*, in the NZM Sept. 1839 supplement; also later, in Leipzig]	piano	1839	1839 (Vienna, Mechetti)
—	"Am Strande" (Burns)	voice and piano	1840	—
—	"Volkslied" (Heine)	voice and piano	1840	—
12	Zwölf Gedichte aus Rückert's Liebesfrühling, von Robert und Clara Schumann [pub. as Robert Schumann, Op. 37] "Er ist gekommen" (1836) "Liebst du um Schönheit" (1841) "Warum willst du andere fragen" (1841)	voice and piano	1841	1841 (Leip, B & H)
—	Sonatina	piano	1841 [–1842?]	—
13	Sechs Lieder "Ich stand in dunklen Träumen" (Heine) (1840) "Sie liebten sich Beide" (Heine) (1842) "Liebeszauber" (Geibel) (1842) "Der Mond kommt still gegangen" (Geibel) (?) "Ich hab' in deinem Auge" (Rückert) (1843) "Die stille Lotosblume" (Geibel) (?)	voice and piano	1840–1843	? (Leip, B & H)
—	"Loreley" (Heine)	voice and piano	1843	—
—	"Oh—weh des scheidens, das er tat" (Heine)	voice and piano	1843	—
14	Deuxième Scherzo	piano	?1841 or 1842	1845 (Leip, B & H)

Op.	Title	scoring	date of composition	date of publication
15	Quatre pièces caractéristiques	piano	?1841 or 1842	1845 (Leip, B & H)
16	Drei Praeludien und Fugen	piano	1845	1846 (Leip, B & H)
17	Trio	piano, vln, cello	by 1846	1847 (Leip, ?B & H)
—	"Beim Abschied" (Serre)	voice and piano	1846	—
—	"Mein Stern" (Serre)	voice and piano	1846	—
—	Concertino, F mi (incomplete)	piano and orchestra	1847	—
—	Part-songs (texts, Geibel) "Abendfeier in Venedig" "Vorwärts" "Gondoliera"	mixed chorus	1848	—
20	Variationen über ein Thema von Robert Schumann, F sharp mi	piano	1853	1854 (Leip, B & H)
21	Drei Romanzen, A mi, F ma, G mi	piano	1853	1855 or 1856 (Leip, B & H)
22	Drei Romanzen, D flat ma, G mi, B flat ma	violin and piano	1853	1855 or 1856 (Leip, B & H)
23	Sechs Lieder aus Jucunde von Rollet "Was weinst du, Blümlein, in Morgenschein?" "An einem lichten Morgen" "Geheimes Flüstern hier und dort" "Auf einem grünem Hügel" "Das ist ein Tag" "O Lust, O Lust vom Berg ein Lied"	voice and piano	1853	1855 or 1856 (Leip, B & H)
—	Marsch in E flat	piano	1879	—
—	"Der Traum"	voice and piano	n.d.	—
—	"Abendstern"	voice and piano	n.d.	—

Cadenzas:
  Beethoven, C minor concerto, Op. 37, first movement
  Beethoven, G major concerto, Op. 58, first and third movements
  Mozart, D minor concerto, K. 466, first and third movements

Quatre Pièces Caractéristiques, Opus 5 (1835-1836)

Impromptu: Le Sabbat

Caprice à la boleros

Romance

Scène fantastique: Le Ballet des Revenants

IMPROMPTU

LE SABBAT.

Die richtige Anwendung des Pedals mit strenger Beobachtung des Harmoniewechsels wird vorausgesetzt, nur an den nöthigsten Stellen ist dasselbe näher bezeichnet.

4

CAPRICE À LA BOLEROS.

No 2.

CLARA WIECK OP.5.

2308

7

CLARA WIECK OP. 5.

2308

11

CLARA WIECK OP.5.

2308

ROMANCE.

N.º 3.

SCÈNE FANTASTIQUE:

LE BALLET DES REVENANTS.

Allegro ma non troppo.

No. 4.

CLARA WIECK OP.5.　　　　　2308

L'istesso tempo.

CLARA WIECK OP.5.

2308

CLARA WIECK OP. 5.

CLARA WIECK OP. 5.

Fine.

SOIRÉES MUSICALES

contenant:

Toccatina, Ballade, Nocturne
Polonaise et deux Mazurkas

pour le

PIANOFORTE

dédiée

à Madame Henriette Voigt

par

CLARA WIECK

Pianiste de la Cour I. et R. Apostolique.

Propriété des Editeurs
Enrégistré aux Archives de l'Union.

Oeuv. 6.   Pr. 20 Gr.

Leipzig, chez Frédéric Hofmeister.
Paris, chez Richault.   Varsovie chez G. Sennewald.

TOCCATINA.

Clara Wieck Op. 6.

Presto.

N⁰ 1.

On présuppose le stricte emploi de la Pédale et ce n'est qu'aux endroits les plus urgents que l'application en est indiquée.

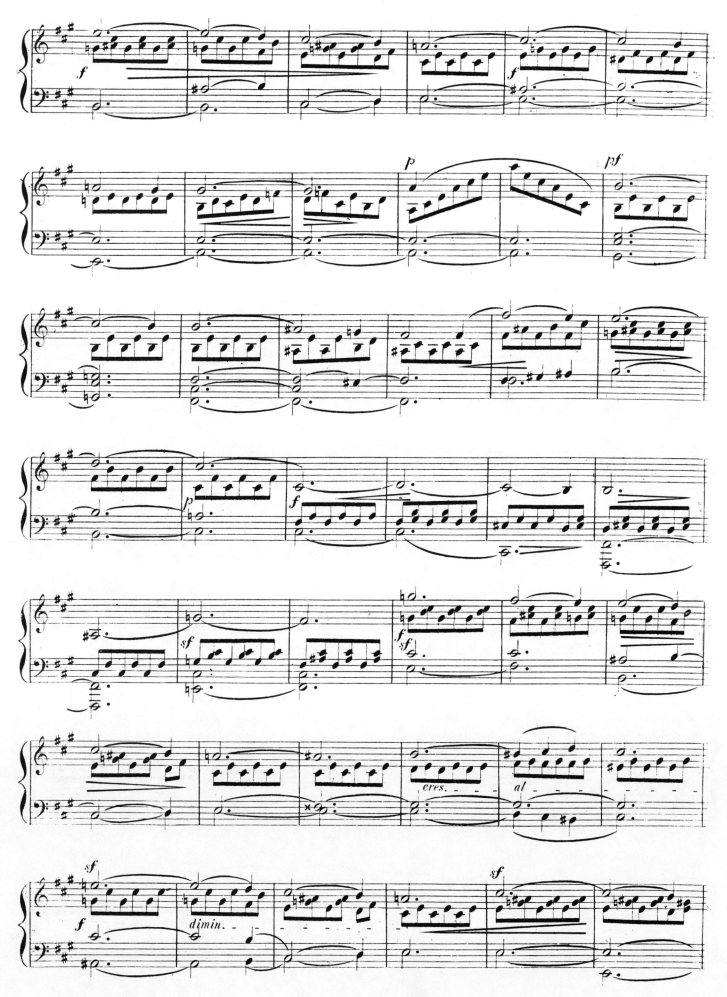

NOTTURNO.

MAZURKA.

BALLADE.

MAZURKA.

POLONAISE.

2148

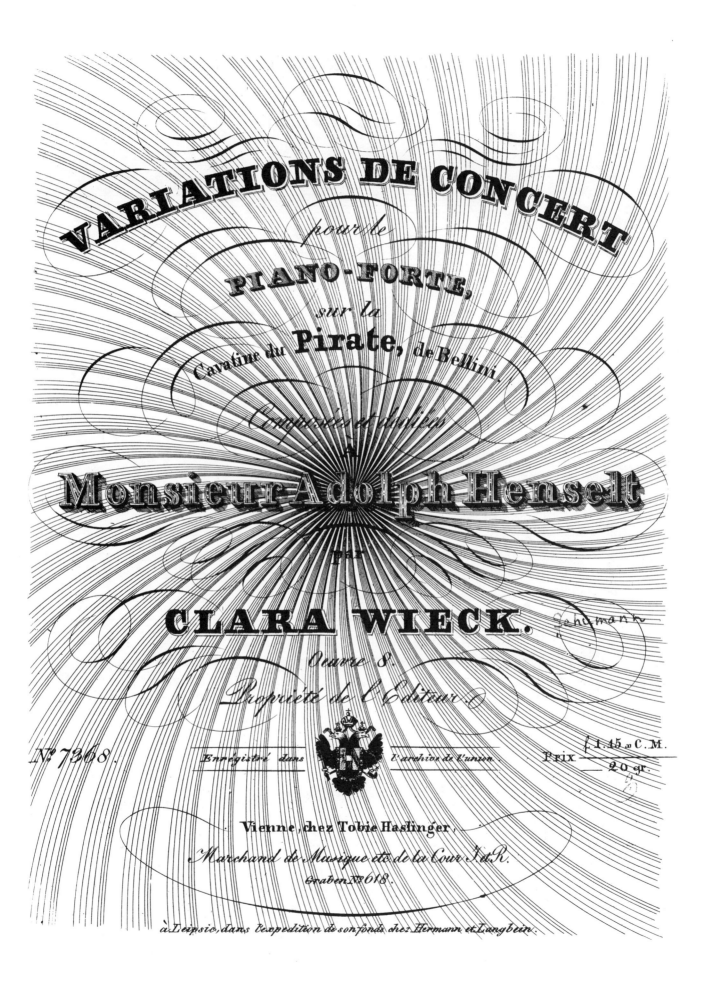

VARIATIONS DE CONCERT
pour le Pianoforte seul
par
CLARA WIECK.
Oeuvre 8.

Introduzione.

Die richtige Anwendung des Pedals mit strenger Beobachtung des Harmoniewechsels wird vorausgesetzt, nur an den nöthigsten Stellen ist dasselbe näher bezeichnet.

(7368.)

Eigenthum und Verlag der k. k. Hof-Kunst- und Musikalienhandlung des Tobias Haslinger in Wien.

4

CAVATINA.

Andantino.
molto espressivo.

p

Pedale.

sempre piano il Basso.

cresc.

ten.

Ped.

mf

ten.

Ped.

stringendo.

cre _ _ scen _ _

T. H. 7368.

T.H.73.

8   Molto grandioso ma non troppo Allegro.

Var. 2.

10

Var.3.

T. H. 7368.

12

Adagio
quasi
Fantasia
à capriccio.

T.H.7368.

14

Brillante e passionato.

Var. 4.

T.H.7368.

16

Volante.

T. H. 7368.

SCHERZO

pour le *Pianoforte*

composé par

CLARA WIECK.

Pianiste de S. M. I. R. l'Impératrice d'Autriche.

Propriété des Editeurs.

Oeuv. 10.   **Pr. 16 Gr.**

LEIPSIC, CHEZ BREITKOPF & HÄRTEL.

Paris, chez Schonenberger.

Nº 5987.

Enrégistré dans l'Archive de l'Union.

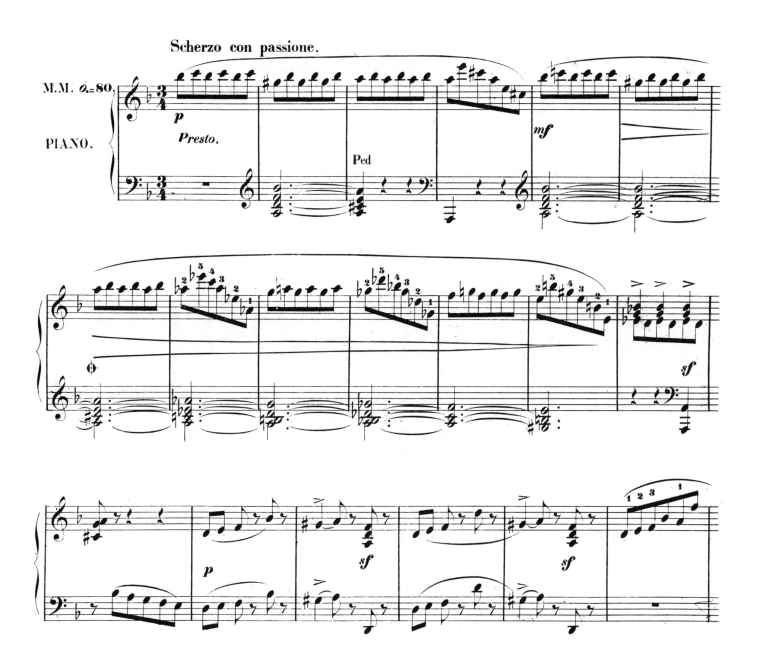

SCHERZO

composé
pour le Pianoforte
par

CLARA WIECK.

Pianiste de S.M. L'Empereur d'Autriche.

Scherzo con passione.

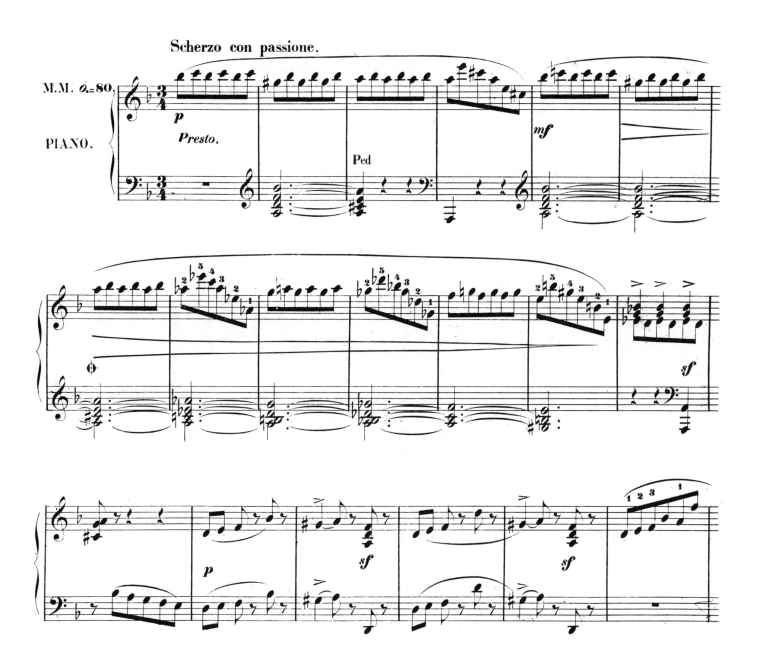

5987.

Leipsic, chez Breitkopf et Härtel. Propriété des Éditeurs. Paris, chez Schonenberger.

4

5987

8

5987

Trois

ROMANCES

pour le

PIANO

dédiées à Monsieur

ROBERT SCHUMANN

par

CLARA WIECK,

Pianiste de S. M. I. R. l'Empereur d'Autriche.

Propriété des Editeurs.
Enregistré dans l'Archive de l'Union.

Oeuvre 11.   Prix 45 x A. d. C.

VIENNE,

chez Pietro Mechetti qm Carlo,

Marchand de Musique et de beaux Arts de la Cour I. et R.
Place St. Michel No 1153.

Paris, chez Simon Richault.

TROIS ROMANCES

par

CLARA WIECK.

Oeuvre 11.

ritardando.

ten.

p

ten.

ritard:

ritard:

ritard:

Nach und nach schneller.

6

Allegro passionato.

Tempo, wie zu Anfang.

8

P. M. Nᵒ 3391.

P.M.Nᵒ 3391.

III
Praeludien und Fugen

für das

PIANOFORTE

componirt

von

CLARA SCHUMANN,
GEB. WIECK,

Kammervirtuosin Sr. Maj. des Kaisers von Oestreich.

Op.16.

Eigenthum der Verleger.

Leipzig, bei Breitkopf & Härtel.

Pr. 25 Ngr.

7334.

Eingetragen in das Vereinsarchiv.

PRAELUDIUM I.

Clara Schumann, Op. 16.

attacca **Fuga**

FUGA I.

Allegro vivace.

PRAELUDIUM II.

Allegretto.

PIANOFORTE.

attacca Fuga

7334

FUGA II.

Andante.

sempre legato.

mf

7334

PRAELUDIUM III.

ritard.

attacca Fuga

7334

FUGA III.

Andante con moto.

Fine.